Politics and Aesthetics

Politics and Aesthetics

Jacques Rancière
Peter Engelmann

Translated by Wieland Hoban

polity

First published in German as *Politik und Ästhetik*, © Passagen Verlag, Ges.m.b.H., Wien, 2016. English language edition published by arrangement with Eulama Lit. Ag.

Author image on page vi © Marina Faust

Polity Press
65 Bridge Street
Cambridge CB2 1UR, UK

Polity Press
101 Station Landing
Suite 300
Medford, MA 02155, USA

ISBN-13: 978-1-5095-3501-9
ISBN-13: 978-1-5095-3502-6 (pb)

A catalogue record for this book is available from the British Library.

Library of Congress Cataloging-in-Publication Data

Names: Ranciere, Jacques, interviewee. | Engelmann, Peter, interviewer.
Title: Politics and aesthetics / Jacques Ranciere, Peter Engelmann.
Other titles: Politik und Asthetik. English
Description: Cambridge, UK ; Medford, MA : Polity Press, [2019] | Translation of: Politik und Asthetik. | Includes bibliographical references and index.
Identifiers: LCCN 2018059986 (print) | LCCN 2019005001 (ebook) | ISBN 9781509535033 (Epub) | ISBN 9781509535019 (hardback) | ISBN 9781509535026 (pbk.)
Subjects: LCSH: Aesthetics--Political aspects. | Political science--Anthropological aspects. | Political psychology.
Classification: LCC BH301.P64 (ebook) | LCC BH301.P64 R3613 2017 (print) | DDC 111/.85--dc23
LC record available at https://lccn.loc.gov/2018059986 or this book is available from the British Library.

Typeset in 12.5 on 15 pt Adobe Garamond by
Servis Filmsetting Ltd, Stockport, Cheshire
Printed and bound in Great Britain by TJ International Limited

For further information on Polity, visit our website: politybooks.com

Contents

First Conversation

Peter Engelmann   I suggest we begin by talking about your intellectual career, which began with Althusser and followed a structuralist approach, though you soon moved away from this. You could describe your political concern and outline your research on the social movements of the nineteenth century, and explain how you proceeded from there to develop a new perspective on politics and art. After that I'd ask you to explain the major lines of your current critical thought and its theoretical foundations.

Jacques Rancière   Agreed.

PE   So let's start from your encounter with Althusser. Perhaps you can talk about how you ended up collaborating on *Reading Capital*,[1] and why you subsequently distanced yourself from that structuralist interpretation of Marx. Or perhaps you want to go even further back?

JR   Well, in 1960 I started at the École Normale Supérieure, where Althusser was teaching at the time. I was a young man who had first become acquainted with Marxism more through reading existentialist or religious texts, because in France it was mainly Jesuits who had written good theoretical texts about Marx.

PE   You were a Jesuit?

JR   I wasn't a Jesuit, but back then there were practically no theoretical texts on Marx that had been written by communists. And the texts with the most detailed commentary on Marx were by Jesuits, especially Père Calvez, who had written a very extensive book entitled *Karl Marx*.[2] It was he who introduced many readers to Marx's thought by trying to uncover its philosophical dimension, taking an interest in the young Marx's beginnings and showing the continuity of his thought. And there was Sartre too, through whom I also became acquainted with communism. Sartre pursued a philosophical, existentialist approach that heavily emphasized the problematics of praxis and alienation. But then I went to the École Normale Supérieure, where Althusser questioned this approach on the grounds that it didn't concentrate on the real Marx. He explained that the young Marx on which the commentaries focused was the ideological, pre-scientific Marx, and that one should abandon this existentialist discourse. That was the moment when structuralism emerged, and Althusser's reading forced me to abandon my first approach to Marx. I had pursued it with great enthusiasm and become something of a specialist in early Marx, and I had also written a final dissertation on the subject. I attended Althusser's seminars on *Capital*, which were intended to show the rupture between the young and the later, mature Marx. Althusser's concern was to rediscover Marx's true theory, which would form the point of departure for rethinking the revolution – but above all to enlighten all the young 'petty bourgeois' who lived in such ignorance of the system's laws that they couldn't help going astray. This insistence on the theory of ideology was at the core of Althusser's thinking. And structuralism reinforced a scientistic reading of ideology theory, namely that all people were trapped in an illusion out of structural necessity, and science was needed in order to free them. I followed this direction, which, in a sense, also corresponded with the position of a young student at an elite university. Essentially there was a kind of Marxist aristocracy back then.

PE At the École Normale Supérieure?

JR Yes. You could say we were the best students, the best philosophers, and Marxists at the same time! We were conscious of our role as the intellectual avant-garde. Then came May 1968, a movement that ensued in a way that totally contradicted Althusser's theory, a movement that consisted of students who should really have been knee-deep in petty bourgeois ideology, with no ability to develop a scientific, Marxist, proletarian consciousness. It was this movement that triggered an enormous subversive movement all over the country, extending to all walks of life. So in 1968 one had the impression of a complete rupture between the Marxist scientistic theory previously adhered to and the reality of this movement, the reality of workers' revolts, people's revolts, youth revolts. From that point on I began to criticize this structuralist Marxism, and all the more so when the University of Vincennes was founded after 1968.

PE   How did this university come into existence?

JR   Essentially, one can say that the state gave the radical leftists and the Marxists a university of their own. A university where one could truly practise Marxist, structuralist, semiological science. Those who were there had two choices: either one played along – and Althusserianism was the theory for entering into this schema, as it were – or one didn't want to be co-opted, and refused to be the Marxist poster-child of bourgeois culture. In my case that led to a critique of all the theoretical preconditions from which people had been proceeding until then. I decided on a critique of Althusser, and of all theories which claimed that Marxist science had to help those people who live in a state of illusion to attain consciousness. Then I told myself that to

5

test my critique I would have to take on a historical study that would allow me to gain a genuine understanding of labour history, and of history from the bottom up. So I set about doing work on the labour archives, about the period in which Marx began to write.

PE   That was in the early seventies?

JR   Yes, that was around 1972, 1973. I thought that there had probably been a wasted opportunity for an encounter, or let's say, a lack of understanding between Marxist tradition and the labour tradition.

PE   You went to the archives and became a historian?

JR   Yes, I actually became a historian.

PE   And you visited archives in France and Amsterdam?

JR   Primarily French archives, later some others too. In Amsterdam I went to the archive of the Institute of Social History, but spent much of my time at the National Archive. I researched in the archive collections of the various utopist groups, especially those of the Saint-Simonists and the Icarian workers. But my great discovery was the documents of Gauny, a carpenter from the nineteenth century who was a Saint-Simonist. As if by a miracle, he left behind boxes full of documents that have survived – and one always says that the voices of the people remain unknown and leave no traces! There were eight boxes at the archive, with texts, letters, poems, the collected writings of a Saint-Simonist carpenter who had experienced the nineteenth century as a writer. Here someone 'from below' had left traces! Proceeding from all these archival collections, especially those of the carpenter, I began to undertake a critique of my own position. I was searching for a true workers' thinking, or people's thinking, whose foundations lay in the culture of the people, the workers. It then became clear to me that the workers' activism had come about through an attempt to liberate themselves from a particular workers' identity that was defined by domination.

PE To become part of the bourgeoisie?

JR   To reach a way of thinking and of perceiving the world where one no longer thinks as a worker, but rather begins to have a share in all forms of culture and thought which the bourgeoisie, the intellectuals and the different factions of the ruling class had hitherto claimed for themselves. What I ultimately discovered was that the class struggle and all conflict phenomena aren't simply a head-on opposition between a class with its culture, its ideology and its interests on the one side and a different class on the other side. Many of these phenomena were essentially problems of boundaries; there was the will of these workers to emerge from a kind of captivity and become fully fledged subjects of a shared world. That was evident on many different levels, for example in the fact that strikes were organized on the basis of argumentation. Suddenly, strikes were no longer just expressions of a balance of power, but became something like assertions of intellectual ability, an ability to argue and to discuss a situation. They proved that it wasn't a matter of being stronger, it was a matter of carrying out sensible actions. It was the same with the will to write poetry, for example. The bourgeoisie, the great writers, said to the workers, 'Write folk songs!'

But the workers wanted to write tragedies, not folk songs. So I was interested in all these phenomena relating to boundaries and transgression.

PE   You discovered that the political struggle, the class struggle, was at once a kind of cultural struggle among those who wanted to be accepted into a culture from which they'd previously been excluded? Is that how one could see your political perspective?

JR   But one shouldn't get too fixated on the concept of culture, which is a rather complicated concept. At any rate, what I actually discovered was this intellectual and aesthetic dimension of class struggles. The class struggle was originally the struggle to gain access to a particular lifeworld (*monde vécu*) from a different lifeworld. That can be expressed in culture, because culture is a form of connection to an existing unity. But what the class struggle really calls into question is one's belonging to a class as the assignment to a particular presence in the world, a particular perception of the world, a particular language. Essentially the class struggle contains the will to emerge from the alleged situation that one thinks as a worker, acts as a worker and sees the world as a worker.

I genuinely think that this dimension, which I called 'aesthetic', is very important. 'Aesthetic' not in the sense of viewing works of art, but rather in the strong sense of one's relationship with the perceived world. That was extremely important for me, and led to a very unusual philosophical habilitation thesis that I published as a book called *Proletarian Nights*.[3] It was a philosophical thesis, yet didn't contain a single philosophical thesis, a single argument. There were only stories, narratives, a kind of montage of letters, poems, workers' newspapers and pamphlets that tried to give an account of this struggle on the boundary between two worlds. This montage tried to render visible the fact that the revolution was, in a sense, first of all an aesthetic, a sensual matter. I called this book *Proletarian Nights* because it seeks to make visible the efforts these people undertook to escape the simplest and most immediate form of coercion that burdened their lives, which dictates that if someone works all day, they have to sleep at night so that they can carry on working the next morning. One could say that the emancipation of the workers begins where the workers decide not to sleep but to do other things: to read, to write, to gather at night. That was a very important point, and it allowed me to define both my view of politics and my view of aesthetics.

PE I remember that this aesthetic aspect was never addressed in East Germany. Being a communist or a socialist was always based on an intellectual construction. One had to follow the programme without any feelings: feelings and culture were considered forms of manipulation.

JR Yes.

PE When did you write your habilitation thesis?

JR In the late seventies. I took the viva in 1980 and published it the following year. It was a very peculiar subject, and I ended up somewhere else entirely. It was a habilitation thesis, but dealt with nothing but stories. It was a subject that neither the philosophers nor the historians wanted.

PE You had a position in Vincennes at the time?

JR   I took a position in Vincennes in 1968. The university was set up in a completely different way, with different hiring procedures from the usual ones where one had to appear before a committee. Instead, a number of heads of department had been selected and they were free to hire the staff they wanted.

PE   And Michel Foucault was one of them?

JR   Yes, he was head of the philosophy department.

PE   Everyone at the philosophy department was appointed in the same way?

JR   Originally everyone in Vincennes was chosen that way, by heads of department who were given a completely free hand to put together their teams. But that was only the case the first time, because it was shortly after May 1968. After that, rules were formulated, which was why later on, when I wanted to get a professorship, I had to appear before the normal university committees, and they made it very clear to me that I, not being a philosopher, had no place there. So I became a professor not of philosophy but of aesthetics, because the philosophy committee consisted of very reactionary people who had been swept aside by 1968, as it were, who had been humiliated by the fame of Derrida, Foucault and Althusser and could now take revenge.

PE It's interesting that aesthetics was significant in that field too.

JR I never had any problems as a teacher in Vincennes. I always taught there without anyone telling me what work to do or demanding an account of what I was doing. Though one did have to appear before a national committee to get the professorship. Now there were two different committees: a philosophy committee, which didn't want me, and an aesthetics committee, which wanted to hire me as a professor. That was in 1990. I stayed in the same place, at the same philosophy department, but as professor of aesthetics and politics. That was the institutional side of things. So essentially I was in a situation where, after following my own path, I tried to see what connection there might be between the path I had taken and issues of philosophy or political philosophy. That gradually led me to draw conclusions from my work with regard to philosophy and what people called political theory. I wrote a number of books, like *The Philosopher and His Poor*,[4] in which I tried to develop a genealogy of the proletarian concept based on Marxist theory or Bourdieu's sociology, and going all the way back to Plato. I wanted to show that philosophy too is based on an original separation of two souls – souls of gold and souls of iron. I tried to investigate the relationship which philosophy had established between three figures in Plato's time: the philosopher, the worker and a third figure whom Plato calls the 'sophist' and Marx the 'petty bourgeois'. It's a figure who supposedly always disturbs the good relationship between those on the right and those on the left, between those on the side of thought and those who stand on the side of labour. So I tried to write a philosophical genealogy of this relationship between the 'head people' and the 'hand people' and a third category of people, who can be sophists, artists, petty bourgeois or ideologues, and who, throughout this entire tradition, bring confusion into the good order of things. That's the subject of my book *The Philosopher and His Poor*.

PE When was it published?

JR 1983. Later on, people started asking me about the connection between my work and politics, to political philosophy and daily political affairs. So I started – slightly against my will – to write about politics, political theory and philosophy and democracy. For roughly ten years I pursued a line of thought that led to *Disagreement*,[5] published in 1995. In that book I tried to translate my work on workers' emancipation back into classical concepts from political philosophy, or to locate it within the relationship between philosophy and politics. The idea of the book developed from three points that form a triangle. One of the corners of the triangle consisted in my investigations of workers' emancipation. The second corner was a study on the origin of political philosophy in Plato and Aristotle. The third was the political and ideological situation of the 1980s and 1990s. That was the time when the Soviet Union collapsed and Fukuyama formulated his theories about the end of history and about universal democracy. In France, it was the start of the consensus, that is, the rapprochement, between the positions of the right and the left, with the growth of a kind of shared economic and political *doxa*. In that situation of consensus, in France especially, there were a number of theories and books – the studies by Luc Ferry and Alain Renaut, for example, who stated that we had finally rid ourselves of the class struggle, the labour movement and all that social business, and could henceforth return to real political philosophy. People at the time referred most of all to Leo Strauss, Hannah Arendt and Aristotle to oppose the topics of social struggle with an emphasis on the common good and coexistence. They presented these Aristotelian themes which had been taken up again by Strauss and Arendt. So it was a situation in which, roughly speaking, we had consensus as state practice on the one hand, and on the other a culture of political consensus which claimed to be returning to true political philosophy – referring back very emphatically to classical philosophy. Ultimately, it boiled down to justifying the most commonplace government actions with brilliant philosophical references. So those were the three corners of the triangle: the emergence of a consensus; classical philosophy, which was used to justify it, and which I suggested reading in a different way; and finally my work on workers' emancipation. Starting from there, I tried to rethink what we call 'political' and to show that politics is not a thinking that considers how to organize the individuals in a community, but rather a dispute about the nature of this community.

In reality, political is dissensual, conflictual; one shouldn't simply understand it as a conflict between groups, but as a conflict of worlds. From the start, as soon as Aristotle defines the political animal, he contrasts human language and the animal's voice. And that's precisely where the fundamental conflict lies: whom does one see as a speaking creature, and who is a noisy animal? That was the whole problematics of workers' emancipation. It was about people who were seen as noisy animals and wanted to make themselves heard as speaking creatures. So I thought it was necessary to rethink the conflict and to locate the essence of the conflict in the origins of political thought itself. I worked through Plato's and Aristotle's theories of democracy once again to show that, since its beginnings, philosophy has tried to convince us that politics is a conflict between two groups; there is one world reserved for those people who are made for politics, and one world for all the rest. I countered that with the argument that politics in the real sense exists precisely when those from the other side participate in it. So there's an entire tradition of political philosophy which asserts that politics is made by people who are qualified to conduct politics. But the opposite is the case: politics begins to exist *with* democracy. What's democracy, if not the fact that people hold power without having any special qualifications to exercise that power? The starting point is the conflict which leads to people with no privilege of birth, of science or of money making themselves heard as the true subject in spite of everything.

PE   That's the beginning of politics?

JR   Yes, that's the beginning of politics. I was interested in the fact that what we call 'political philosophy' was always a way to put an end to this beginning, and to shift things back to their rightful places.

PE   And that's been the case since Plato?

JR   Yes, since Plato. Plato tries to justify the

power of those who are qualified to govern the state. For me, the original problem of political philosophy and the tradition of what one calls 'political' lies in the liquidation of democracy. Because democracy is the power of all, no matter who they are, the power of the people who have nothing. Democracy is the true politics, because politics begins precisely when the people whom one assumes are not made for it start taking care of the community's concerns, making decisions, explaining and showing that they can do it, that they have the ability to do it. Our modern governments essentially rest on the idea that power belongs to everyone, that there is an ability possessed by everyone; at the same time, this idea is only invoked to confer power on people who supposedly have the ability to command, to know.

PE Is that the basis for your critique of representative democracy?

JR Not quite. I said that democracy exists when a power is asserted which is the power of all, no matter who they are; the origin of the representative system, on the other hand, lies in the fact that the monarchist, aristocratic system included a representation of those who allegedly had the ability to participate in community matters. In France, for example, there was the monarchy and the so-called estates, that is, groups like the nobility and the clergy, which were supposedly representative. They didn't represent the populace but a class, a force that had a say in community matters. Democracy and representation originally followed completely separate logic. Democracy is the power of all, no matter who they are, which was expressed especially in the principle of drawing lots for public offices in Attic democracy. At the start of Attic democracy, offices were held for very short periods of six months or a year, with very frequent renewal. The lot determined who took a particular office. I don't make any value judgement about that, I simply point out what the original principle of democracy was. The principle of representation is an aristocratic principle which states that there are certain social classes which have more weight than others, and must be represented. That still existed in the nineteenth century in the form of census suffrage, in which only those who paid a certain amount of taxes were allowed to vote. Modern universal suffrage is a compromise between these two principles, which are antagonistic principles. Ultimately, the question is in what direction this relationship takes effect, whether it acts in favour of the ability of all, no matter who they are, or does the opposite, favouring the reproduction of those people who presume themselves to be able and competent to control the affairs of the community.

PE You say that the principle of democracy was based on leaving the allocation of political functions to chance by drawing lots. Is that system still feasible in a more complex world? Take nuclear facilities: can one control or guarantee the security of such facilities on the basis of this principle?

JR I think that control over technology and decision-making power in the name of the community are two completely different things. Let's take France as an example, where each former president is supposedly meant to initiate the new one into the secrets of the nuclear weapons code. That's purely formal: neither one of them actually controls the technical processes any more than we do. The increasing complexity of the sciences and technology is not directly connected to what the government calls competencies, because ultimately no one knows where the competence of our rulers comes from. One could say that their primary competence is the competence of people who have succeeded in acting cleverly inside their party, first and foremost by driving out the rivals within the party. So the competence of these people is in no way more valuable than the competencies one needs to practise all sorts of other professions.

PE   I completely agree with you. Every day we witness the incompetence of politicians who hold public office and purport to be competent in the areas for which they are responsible. Nonetheless, if we leave aside the complexity of our technology, there's still the complexity of our social organization. I myself wouldn't be able to make any decisions about areas that are important for the life of the community. But maybe those are two different things?

JR   Yes, those are two different things. If one looks at what's happening in many very complex organizations nowadays, it becomes clear that they're often run by people who are there because they're close to power and have influence. All these complex organizations ultimately function thanks to the knowledge of those who work there. I have a son who worked for the French railway company for a while, so for a giant machinery. Now all of these machineries are usually run, even in the private sector, by people who are friends of power. The power changes, but this form of complicity doesn't change. And all these organizations would be thrown into a complete state of disaster if the people at the lower levels didn't do their work properly. One has to see that. In a sense, the democracy of intelligences is realized in actual practice. It gets covered up by the social hierarchy, but it exists in actual practice. Because all these big organizations only function thanks to the competencies that exist at all levels of the hierarchy – except, often enough, at the top.

PE I'm not sure I follow you; you mean that there's a democratic principle in all these organizations?

JR All these organizations function thanks to the spread of abilities among all those who work in the organizations, often at the middle or lower levels.

PE They're specialists . . .

JR Yes, they're specialists in administration, bookkeeping, technology. Complex organizations function primarily through this knowledge, which isn't management knowledge but technical knowledge, and through people taking responsibility at all levels. Very often it's not the highest level that coordinates, guides and keeps everything running.

PE But at the same time, it's this highest level that makes decisions if there's a crisis, with far-reaching consequences . . .

JR Yes, in a certain sense they too confirm the thesis that sounds so scandalous when I utter it; namely that the real political power is the power of the 'incompetents', that is, the power of people who have no special competence. They involuntarily confirm the thesis that there is no such thing as genuine political competence. They too practise the competence of the incompetent.

Essentially, the question is who the 'incompetent' are who should govern, which ultimately means whether the power of the incompetent is the broad power of the collective intelligence spread throughout society, or rather the power of a small group of people whose main competence is that of having the means to attain power.

PE Let's get back to democracy, to the beginnings of democracy with its principle of distributing public offices and to the rejection of a principle of representation. Your view is that democracy came from the people, from people without specific competencies.

JR Those are indeed the origins of democracy. Historically speaking, democracy began with the abolition of aristocratic privileges. In Athens there was initially a tradition in which power was held by families who were considered original, autochthonous, who were supposedly descended from some god (*laughs*). Democracy began with the undoing of their power, with the denial of their descent, their property, their social status, and with the assertion of a power that was the power of all, no matter who they were. That's all

I'm saying, and here too, I'm not setting up any norms. I'm trying to find out what these concepts mean, and that was why I went back in history. If one wants to understand democracy, one mustn't start from the speeches of contemporary political representatives who purport to embody democracy; one must try to trace their genealogy and to recognize that what we call democracy is, in reality, a combination of two principles: a democratic principle and an oligarchic principle.

PE What characterizes the oligarchic principle?

JR One could say that the oligarchic principle is the principle of a permanent confiscation of democracy. It's more the principle of what I have called 'police'.

PE So then politics is a concept that belongs in the democratic milieu?

JR It's not a matter of milieu. For politics to exist, there first has to be a specific form of power, a principle of power, that constitutes something other than the power of the master over his slaves, the boss over his workers, the head of the family over his family, the teacher over his students. There has to be a form of power that differs from all other forms of power: economic, familial, pedagogical and so forth. Now the democratic principle is the only one that embodies this demand of politics – a power that constitutes the power of all, no matter who they are, which is a completely unique force precisely because it is not the power of a particular class, a particular authority. So one can say that the democratic principle and the political principle merge into each other. Only the democratic principle, that is, the principle of a rule of all, no matter who they are, corresponds to the idea of a pure political power. All powers that exist are, in reality, mixtures of this power of all, no matter who they are, with powers of descent, of wealth, of knowledge or of a particular caste that reproduces itself.

PE So we're dealing with two different principles and two different ways of functioning, but they exist at the same time?

JR . . .which always mix, sometimes more and sometimes less. That's why, for democracy truly to exist, there have to be people's authorities in the current regimes which are autonomous in relation to the regime of representation.

PE So you develop a conception of democracy and politics directed against the oligarchic logics that threaten democracy and politics from the start?

JR Yes, one could put it like that. One could say that the existence of politics is always conflictual, and never based on anything like consensual organization or delegation. We live under regimes that purport to be regimes of consensual delegation, but in reality what we call 'politics' is a conflict between two antagonistic principles. As in every conflict, the advantage can lie on one side or the other.

PE So you're suggesting a model opposed to that of current politics, and to what one usually means by the word 'politics'. There's a second important element in your thought, namely aesthetics. Just as you established a new definition of politics, you also suggested a new perspective on art and aesthetics. Before we bring these two areas together, let's trace the development of your aesthetic perspective a little.

JR   If one wants to attempt a genealogy of all that, one has to go back to the work on workers' emancipation that I pursued in the seventies. In that work, I developed something from this emancipation which I called the aesthetic dimension, the striving to live in a different sensual world. I commented most of all on the texts of the carpenter Gauny, in which he describes his working day in a splendid villa where he's laying a parquet floor. He's in a situation of class struggle, one could say: he's selling the labour of his hands to provide a boss with profit and an owner with something useful. And there's a moment in his description when he says that he moves his gaze away from the work of his hands. His gaze wanders to the window and takes in the perspective, the buildings, the gardens around him. It's essentially something like Kant's disinterested gaze. For me that was the concrete application of Kant's disinterested gaze, it's certainly not the aesthete's gaze at a beautiful painting, which forgets the class struggle. On the contrary: in a sense, the class struggle begins with the ability of the gaze to separate itself from the hands; that is, the worker makes themselves the material, concrete, aesthetic owner of this world in which they sell their labour power. My thought is that emancipation already begins there. This form of appropriation presupposes that one changes one's gaze, that the gaze is no longer there simply to accompany the work of the hands, but rather goes in a different direction. That's also connected to a dissociation of the body. There's a worker's body, which is made for a particular thing, namely to sell one's labour every day, make a living, sleep at night, rest and then start again the next day. At a certain point, however, this body is dissociated, the gaze separates from the hands, and the worker's body takes on the gaze of an aesthete, the thinking of an aesthete. This also means that the hand will ultimately change its function; it will start writing, writing poems, writing texts.

This attainment of a disinterested aesthetic practice gives a completely new meaning to the canonical texts of aesthetics. Let's recall that in the second paragraph of the *Critique of Judgement*, Kant examines the way in which the exterior of a palace should be viewed in order to reach an aesthetic judgement. He says one can point out that this palace was built with the sweat of the people and for the vanity of the rich, but that the aesthetic judgement consists in leaving this aside, adopting a disinterested gaze and asking oneself if one finds this palace pleasing or not. In a sense, this is what happens to the gaze of the worker who mentally takes possession of the space surrounding them. That's an important point, especially as I was writing *Proletarian Nights* when Bourdieu's *Distinction* came out, a book that had enormous influence.[6] *Distinction* explains that the idea of the aesthetic judgement is simply the consecration of bourgeois taste as free taste, and that working people can only have a taste born of necessity. In Bourdieu's view, the free aesthetic judgement is a privilege of the bourgeois, the intellectual, the aesthete. Consequently, aesthetics is a form of grand mystification which seeks to make people forget that every class has judgements, modes of perception and attitudes that are determined by its situation. For me, Bourdieu's thesis is essentially the same as Plato's thesis that every person, with their own way of being, should stay on the side where their conditions have put them. So emancipation begins when people decide not to stay on their side anymore. Bourdieu's thesis of the radical opposition of tastes along class lines, and hence the thesis that the aesthetic judgement is no more than a philosophical mystification to fool the petty bourgeoisie and give them the illusion of having a share in the universal, was highly influential.

PE You, on the other hand, didn't agree with Bourdieu's argumentation.

JR No, because his thesis completely contradicted what my work on workers' emancipation had taught me, namely that reaching an aesthetic attitude is the basis for the possibility of social upheaval, as it marks the beginning of the emergence from the sensual situation in which the people are imprisoned. So it was very important to me to understand this fact. Around that time, I was in a second-hand bookshop one day and by coincidence – because coincidence has always played an important part in my life – I stumbled on a book by Schiller that I didn't know: *On the Aesthetic Education of Man.* The significance of these letters, which were published in 1795, in the middle of the French Revolution, lies in the fact that they put the whole of Kantian aesthetics into a kind of political perspective. It wasn't a book in favour of the revolution, but it did insist on what one could call the egalitarian dimension of aesthetic experience, on the idea of creating a new form of humanity on the basis of a kind of revolution of the senses. The definition of the sensual ability that Schiller calls 'ludic drive' [*Spieltrieb*] leads to the ruin of the old hierarchy, because the hierarchies between intelligence and sensuality or form and matter are, in a sense, symbolizations of a social hierarchy in which there are culture people on the one hand and nature people on the other, people of reason on one side and people of emotion on the other. That's my own reading of Schiller, of course, which comes from the side of experience, the side of workers' emancipation. From there, I reflected on what was going on during this aesthetic revolution at the end of the eighteenth century.

This political dimension of the aesthetic played an important part in my thinking. Aesthetics isn't the theory of art, the theory of beauty, the observation of beauty. 'Aesthetics' defines itself first of all as a way of experiencing a sensory state which has abandoned the hierarchies that normally organize sensory experience, such as the hierarchy between sensuality, which receives, and the mind, which organizes; or between intelligence, which determines, and the hands, which obey. One can say that these hierarchical ways of organizing experience are at once political and social forms. This very important principle underlies the connection between aesthetics and politics that I have tried to describe. From that moment, I thought that the aesthetic is not a theory of art or beauty, but rather an entire regime of experience. I connected two things: the idea of aesthetic experience as egalitarian experience and what I have called the 'regime of identifying art'. This distinction between regimes became increasingly evident while working on the threshold between literature and history. For example, one speaks very generally of 'literature', but literature is actually a recent concept that appeared around the transition from the eighteenth to the nineteenth century and served the purpose of viewing the works that were created or conceived in other categories – those of poetry or rhetoric. In the same way, one speaks very generally of 'art', but the concept of art as we use it is one that probably didn't exist before the end of the eighteenth century. One says that Plato excluded art, but

Plato doesn't exclude art – Plato doesn't know art. Plato knows arts, *technai*, and he decides which are good and which are not, how they should be applied and what purposes they should serve. Before the concept of art in the singular appeared, there was a distinction between types of art, of technique, of knowledge – especially the contrast between the free arts and the mechanical arts, and this contrast in fact relates not to the content of the arts, but fundamentally to the kind of people practising the arts.

PE   Is that where the real distinction lies?

JR   Let's say, the old distinction was based on the kind of person who was assigned one activity or another. To come back to Aristotle again: in Book Eight of the *Politics*, he explains very well that there are activities which are bad for free men because they deform the body, but also because they are too specialized. For example, he says that a free man mustn't practise an art too skilfully, because that would amount to a profession – and a profession is suitable for an artisan, but not a free man. So I pointed out that the fine arts are essentially heirs of the free arts, which are primarily activities fit for free people, people with free time – in contrast to all the artisanal activities, which are occupational activities. These sensual and social separations were simultaneously the reason why art didn't exist as a general category, as it does today. If one considers things from a historical perspective, it becomes clear that there are essentially three possible attitudes towards what we call a work of art, for example a Greek statue.

First of all, one can view it as the image of a god. Then one asks oneself if one has the right to make statues or depictions of the gods. One knows that the answer could be negative. And one also asks oneself if this image represents the god and his attributes well, and expresses a good doctrine. I call that the *ethical regime* of images; one finds it in Plato, but it also showed itself when the Taliban destroyed the Buddhas of Bamiyan. Some people called them part of humanity's world cultural heritage, but for the Taliban they were images, idols that one treats the same way as Christians treated statues of gods or the Protestants treated Catholic images: one destroys them.

In the second regime, which I call the *repre-*

sentative regime, one decides that there are forms of imitation which are legitimate in their field, which have their own legitimacy. When Aristotle wrote the *Poetics* or the authors of the seventeenth and eighteenth centuries wrote treatises on the poetic arts, what else were they doing but creating a kind of law, a law of imitations that dictates what a poem should be like, what a work of art should be like, why and how one should make it, what audience one makes it for, what feeling it's meant to evoke. So there's a kind of legislation which goes back at least as far as Aristotle, but also has contemporary forms – especially for those arts which address themselves to a larger audience, as they say. It's a legislation that one can call normative, it dictates which purposes the works must obey in order to be works of art. Voltaire, for example, in the eighteenth century, took every single tragedy by Corneille, criticized its scenes and said, here the prince isn't behaving the way a prince should, there the princess is acting like a chambermaid, or there the general isn't speaking the way a general should speak. Or take the Hollywood producer of the twentieth and twenty-first centuries: he stands in front of his screenplay or his film; he organizes previews

with a representative audience and cuts out whatever he feels doesn't correspond to the sensuality
and expectations of his audience. That's what I
call a representative regime: a regime in which
there's a form of legitimacy, and thus a form of
legislation.

PE   In what way does the representative regime
define the representative dimension of a work of
art and its legitimacy?

JR   In the representative regime, a statue is a
depiction that one will judge with reference to
a number of internal norms, but these norms
always supposedly represent the sensuality of an
audience. That's ultimately why the so-called
classical representative regime is always based
on the idea of a human nature. Obviously this
human nature is in reality the nature of a selected
and restricted audience, but this regime is always
based on the idea that the rules of art correspond
to the laws that guide sensuality. A representative film proceeds from the idea that a work of
art is an imitation, but an imitation isn't simply
a copy; it possesses an autonomy. Aristotle, for
example, says that a tragedy is a succession of

actions that follows necessities or probabilities. In the Renaissance, for example, the art of writing was the dominant art which painting took as its model. Therefore, a painting had to be structured in a similar way to a plot and obey certain rules of disposition and proportion. And in the eighteenth century, the question arose whether dance should be taken up into the ranks of the arts, whether it tells a story, whether it's a succession of actions and causes. One can call that the logic of representation, which is a logic in the autonomous sense, but at once remains very closely tied to a hierarchical order of the world. This regime is based on an idea of what is supposed to be depicted, how and for whom, and what form it should take. One could think of the classical theories of drama, for example, and their distinction between tragedy and comedy, which is based on the fact that tragedy depicts nobles and comedy ordinary people. Or one looks at the hierarchy among types of painting in the eighteenth century: history painting was at the top and genre painting right at the bottom. Here we see once again that the differences aren't technical, but that the hierarchy corresponds to the hierarchy of the subjects, that is, that there is really a very close connection between an artistic hierarchy and a political or social one. That characterizes the representative regime.

Then I analysed what happened over a longer period, between the end of the eighteenth century and the start of the nineteenth. One can say that this period saw the birth of what I call the *aesthetic regime*. It's a regime in which the entire hierarchical order of representation is questioned and this leads to a paradoxical situation. The paradox is that the aesthetic regime will define a specific sphere of art in which the arts no longer exist, but rather art. That begins with Winckelmann's *History of the Art of Antiquity*. A title like *History of the Art of Antiquity* sounds banal, but it was the first time that anyone spoke of the 'history of art' in the singular. Before that there were histories of artists, somewhat in the manner of Plutarch, histories of great men, moralizing histories of great personalities, but no history of art. So, suddenly, art appeared as a concept in the singular that defined a sphere of specific experience which no longer obeys the same rules as other spheres of experience. It was also the time in which people began to exhibit paintings in museums simply as paintings, the portrait of a prince or a scene belonging to this or that genre. It was the time in which there would be rooms full of Italian paintings, of Dutch paintings, presented quite simply as paintings. Essentially, the works of art were freed from their function of illustrating faith, showing the greatness of great men, decorating their palaces. This enabled the emergence of art in the true sense, but at the same time, because one was no longer in the representative dispositif, there were no more norms to dictate what was a good or bad artistic subject, what should or should not be accepted into the ranks of art.

As long as one is operating within a representative legislation, one can decide what isn't art. In the aesthetic regime, however, though art suddenly exists as a sphere of experience, there is now no longer a criterion for acceptance, one could say. Gradually one arrives at the situation we know today: anything can be taken up into art. At the start of the nineteenth century, people echoed Wordsworth's statement that the intimate feelings of a farmer are just as interesting as the feelings of a noble lady. Speaking of Murillo's beggar boys, Hegel called it an ideal painting on the grounds that these little beggars enjoyed the same freedom as the gods of Olympus. Flaubert would later say that there is no such thing as noble subject matter – that there is no subject matter at all, in fact. Then all the forms of painting developed that were closely connected to the simple pleasures of the people. Gradually, as we know, everything found its way into the museums; one arrived at the point where people complained that one could find all manner of things in the museums – buckets of glue, heaps of coal, cans of soup, whatever! In a sense, I try to show that there is a fundamental logic of the work in all this. So I'm not in agreement with the great distinctions between an 'explosion of modernity' around 1900 on the one hand, which resulted in the end of representation, in the autonomy of the work and in *medium specificity*, and the 'collapse of classical modernity' in the 1960s on the other hand, Pop Art, the breaking-down of the boundary between great art and popular or commercial art, and so on. I don't agree with that analysis. It's the same underlying logic at work, the logic of a regime characterized by a fundamental tension between the existence of art as its own mode of experience on the one hand, and the possibility that anything can become a work of art on the other hand. I try to question the established opinions on modernity and postmodernity. In the case of abstract painting, the existence of an abstract painting is preceded by the existence of an abstract view of painting as a condition. An abstract view of painting initially developed in the art criticism of the nineteenth century, a view that forgets the narrative of the painting, the subject matter, in order to regard the painting as a totality of events of painterly material. If an abstract painting is possible, it's the result of this process. At the same time, one sees that this abstract painting is only one form among many other forms that became possible through this transformation of one's view. So one can't say that the appearance of Kandinsky's or Malevich's abstract compositions marked a radical historical rupture.

PE So your analysis doesn't correspond to the classic pattern of art-historical periodization, the established definition of modernity and the separation of modernity from postmodernity. Could you explain your periodization more precisely against this background, with reference to the distinction between the representative and aesthetic regimes?

JR   One can say that the representative regime began to develop with Aristotle's *Poetics*, that it renewed itself with all the poetics and treatises that were written in the Renaissance, and was consecrated in the seventeenth and eighteenth centuries with the formulation of veritable laws of imitation, a classification of forms and an entire set of rules. One can say that this regime defined the laws of what one called the fine arts and literature. At any rate, the aesthetic regime set itself apart from the representative regime by defining a rupture, with the result that on the one hand there was henceforth art rather than the fine arts, but on the other hand there were no more norms to decide what belonged to art and what didn't. That brought the reign of the representative order to an end. The modern schema, in the Greenbergian sense, identifies representation and figuration, but that doesn't apply. Representation is not figuration. Representation is essentially a hierarchical logic which states that we are allowed to depict one thing but not another, and that one should depict actions or figures in accordance with the forms that are suited to them – to reserve tragedy for great men and comedy for the common people, for example, or genre painting for the peasants and great history painting for the nobility. That defines the representative order, which was questioned. It declined very slowly, starting in the late eighteenth century. In my opinion, that's what characterizes representation, and it has nothing to do with the reductive opposition of figuration and abstraction.

In the course of the nineteenth century, an abstract view developed bit by bit, an aesthetic view of works that are figurative, created within the framework of representative logic. One has to understand that in the nineteenth century people were starting to look especially at works from the seventeenth century in a new way. Recall all the commentaries by art critics who travelled to the Netherlands. They looked at the paintings by Rubens, by Rembrandt, and they saw them with new eyes: no longer as depictions of this or that subject matter, but as something like events in painterly material. I think that the anti-representative revolution began at that time, not between 1910 and 1920, when people started painting abstract pictures. It took place very slowly, starting at the end of the eighteenth century, with the transformation of the view, including the view of works from the past, because the aesthetic regime is a regime in which one sees the works of the past in a new, different way.

I also examined the question of the realist novel from this perspective. The simplistic modernity that arose in the forties viewed the novel of the nineteenth century as an apologist for representative logic – because it's realistic. I would argue that the opposite is true, because from the exact moment when one accords the same significance to a peasant girl as to a princess, one is no longer in the representative regime. One special trait of the nineteenth-century novel is a form of descriptive focalization that no longer has anything to do with the representative order, the view from above. One sees that in all the criticisms from the reactionaries of the nineteenth century, who complained that the writers were dealing with little things and describing little people. There's a text by a critic of Flaubert who expresses his disgust at how much time Flaubert spends telling the stories of all these lowly people, and instead praises the novel of former times, of the seventeenth century, which was for noble people and depicted noble people whom the common folk only ever saw through the windows of their carriages. One descends from the carriage, somewhat like the way Mao says that one dismounts from a horse, and enters the life of the people, which also presupposes a kind of focalization, of closer view, which already amounts to the collapse of the proportions of the representative order. Contrary to the prevailing opinion, then, the realism of the nineteenth century was by no means an apologist for the representative order. It was its collapse, because it was the collapse of all the proportions and conventions on which that order was based.

PE Now I'd be interested to hear how the relationship between aesthetics and politics is envisaged in the respective art regimes.

JR I tried to show that the aesthetic regime is a paradoxical regime from the start, because, on the one hand, it defines something like a specific sphere of art, and on the other hand, it destroys any boundary between this aesthetic sphere and the sphere of life in general – hence this double tension that exists in the aesthetic regime. The idea that art creates its own unique sphere, with its own laws and its own mode of existence, was contained in Schiller's idea of the aesthetic education of man from the start. He developed the idea of a kind of vocation, a form of aesthetic experience that is destined to become something like a form of holistic experience of life, and even of coexistence. One sees how the idea of an aesthetic education of humanity appeared here, and one sees how it was immediately taken up by Hegel, Schelling and Hölderlin when they wrote *The Oldest Systematic Programme of German Idealism*. They defined something like the programme for an aesthetic revolution, the unification of philosophy and the people; they formulated a kind of embodiment of thought in the sensual forms of collective existence and placed them in opposition to the idea of the state, the organization of collective life by the state. One also finds this idea in Marx's early texts, where he argues for the human revolution against the political revolution. Essentially, this is the idea that there is a sensual constitution of the community that opposes the organization of the community via the state, via legislation and decrees. It returned with great force in the early twentieth century, especially in the art of the Soviet avant-garde.

So, contrary to the notion of modernity as a separation of art and everyday experience, one sees that the idea begins to emerge of an identity between the forms which produce art and the forms of a new collective life. I tried to show that especially using Dziga Vertov's film *Man with a Movie Camera*, as well as the posters that were used to advertise the film.[7] One sees how a form of art appears which no longer defines itself as a creation intended for consumption by individuals, but as identical to a new community's forms of constitution. Here one sees the contrast between aesthetic logic and representative logic: those whom one calls artists of the avant-garde don't want to make art in the service of politics or create works of art, but rather create forms of life. Vertov's film sees itself not as an instrument in the service of a political line, in the service of communism, but as something that's already an expression of communism in sensual terms, proceeding from all the everyday activities that are connected via montage and will form a sort of communal, egalitarian and dynamic fabric of sensual life. So what does one see here? The Soviet authorities will say this is formalism, and demand that artists create works which are in the service of the party, depict real problems of life and help people recover from their work. So, on the one side there's a form of art that wants to break down the boundaries between art and life, art and politics, work and recreation, leisure and work – that's aesthetic logic – and on the other side we have representative logic, the logic of those who lead and who say that art is a special practice, and that artists must place themselves in the service of political goals which are set elsewhere.

PE The communist party follows representative logic?

JR Yes, absolutely. Whereas communist artists follow aesthetic logic. They inscribe themselves into a continuity which transcends the differences between economic and state forms. The idea of aesthetic education has led to numerous interpretations. Hölderlin spoke of an aesthetic church – we can assume that, at the time, he probably meant a small community of the elect. Then throughout the nineteenth century there was genuinely the idea of a new form of revolution, one that wasn't simply a change of government, of laws, but really the constitution of a form of sensual, collective fabric of community. The idea that the revolution isn't simply a change of government, of laws, of institutions, but a transformation of the forms of perception, of activity, of emotions, is one that arose repeatedly between the late nineteenth century and the early twentieth century as an attempt to conceive of the forms of art as new forms of existence. That's not unique to the Soviet revolution, but the Soviet artists played a major part in it, because they had the feeling that they were truly creating a new, communal world. Essentially they were following the idea of aesthetic revolution, the idea that would give them their role within incipient communism. It's the idea that the revolution is above all a revolution of the forms of life, of the sensual universe, and of how to perceive it and act within it. That's why I emphasized the importance of the connection to space, the role of the angled line, the diagonal, as a suspension of the relationship between above and below, and at the same time, a form of spatial pointer that's already directed at the future and has been absorbed by its time.

So one reaches a point where there's an artistic avant-garde that isn't an avant-garde in the military sense – people marching forwards – but rather consists of people seeking to create a sensual reality of communism, in a world where the party says that communism will come in five, ten, fifteen, thirty, fifty, two hundred years as long as one follows the plans correctly and if the party's strategy of gradually creating the material conditions for communism succeeds. On the one side, strategic logic says that one has to create the material foundation for communism first, and on the other side, aesthetic logic says that to get there, communism must always already be there and exist as a way of experiencing sensual perception. Soviet artists tried to create this mode of experience in a very ambiguous way. In Vertov's *Man with a Movie Camera*, for example, the everyday activities in a city are composed together to form a great symphony of movement. So at the end of the film, this great symphony of movement, which is the symphony of new life, is presented in the evening in a cinema to those who appeared in it: they are shown the ordinary activities which they carried out during the day as the living reality of communism. They watch it like an audience, with a somewhat ambiguous gaze, where one wonders if they're aware of setting up communism, or if they're amused by the thought that they're setting up communism. I tried to emphasize that ambiguity.

PE   Does theoretical communism belong to a revolutionized regime?

JR   In a sense, communism is a combination of two logics. A representative logic, where one first has to create the foundation of communism – the coming communism as a result of consistently following the right path. At the same time, in the idea of communism found in the early texts of Marx, one finds the idea that in communism one is no longer in a regime that separates means and ends. What characterizes the old order in these early texts by Marx? That labour is not a way of perfecting the essence of the human being, because labour in capitalism is simply a way to earn a living. At the same time, one can say that people don't realize their essence in their everyday activities, so one locates the essence of the human elsewhere: in religion, in the state and in other forms of alienation. The idea of revolution is the idea of eliminating this relationship of externality between ends and means, and ensuring that the essence of the community is already realized now in everyday activities. In a sense, the idea of communism consists in the fact of people directly realizing the principle of human community in their everyday activity, whereas, from a strategic perspective, that might only happen in billions of years, as Mao says. For the Soviet artists, it already exists now in a certain sense. The everyday activities that Vertov filmed and put together already constitute, very simply and factually, the essence of community realized in everyday activity. With regard to Vertov's film, one can say on the one hand that communism is already there, and on the other hand, that it's there, but only as theatre.

PE   The artists realize this early Marxian idea.

JR   You could say that.

PE   The people don't.

JR   Yes and no; because the artist depicts the activities of everyone, no matter who they are. Before that film, Vertov had made one called *A Sixth Part of the World*, which consists mostly of pictures that were made in Asia, and which show people who aren't modern at all – goatherds in the furthest reaches of Asia, nomads in the steppes of the north, or Eskimos. He takes all these disparate activities of workers, farmers, nomads, shepherds, hunters, and puts them together. These activities, the activities of everyone, become the sensual fabric of communism. So the people is not the authority that's already there, which the artists find; instead, there's an activity which is the activity of all. One could say that the artist views themselves simply as the one who puts all these activities together to show that all of them, arranged together, already form the reality of a new world.

PE   So one can find embodiments of this idea, or this reality, everywhere?

JR   Yes, one can say that.

PE   But the reality for the majority of people in the Soviet Union was a different one; there was civil war from the start . . .

JR   Yes, there was civil war from the start, but when it finished, with the New Economic Policy (NEP), a situation came about in which it was no longer the fighting people in the foreground, but rather multiplicity, the mosaic of activities that one can put together to show communism as a living reality. They were no longer in the time of the civil war, they were in the time of the struggle for production.

PE Was the struggle for production experienced in other ways?

JR One can think of the struggle for production in different ways: in the form of instructions that were given by the party and passed on to the base, or, as in these films, as a symphony of movement.

PE I think one could also find documents which show that the people genuinely experienced production in this different way. I sensed that too during my childhood, in that idealistic period in East Germany.

JR That's precisely why it's uninteresting to conceive of it simply in terms of manipulation and illusion. In a sense, there's a continuity to my work in that, in the critique of a particular idea of illusion. One can always say that life is an illusion, but at the same time, one passes through a large number of sensual states in which one actually perceives the world in different ways. Hence aesthetic freedom, the famous aesthetic freedom, isn't just the freedom of the neoliberal subject; it's a form of concrete experience. Even if one can always say afterwards that a form of concrete experience is illusory, it doesn't change the fact that it was always concretely undergone as experience. One has to be standing on the outside to be able to say that it's merely illusion, manipulation, semblance.

PE   So are you trying to preserve, or recover, the memory of the experiences which people had, in their specific particularity?

JR   Yes, one can say that I'm trying to preserve the reality of that experience. Because, in spite of everything, the reality of what people experience can't be reduced to the explanation for this experience that one tries to supply. In spite of everything, history is made from what people really do, try out and feel. Afterwards, when one looks at a period of twenty or thirty years, one can always show that what they did served this or that cause, and that they weren't doing what they thought they were at all. But those explanations aren't ultimately interesting. What's always interesting is to reveal the potential, the ability, that's at work in these forms of experience. And that's what I try to do in my analysis of workers' emancipation when I reflect on all these experiences: I try to preserve the positive element, the emancipatory potential, the fact that people are living differently. Let me repeat: in that work, I don't simply view workers' emancipation as the fact of fighting for a better future, but as the fact of already living a different present.

PE Emancipation isn't limited to the individual worker?

JR Of course not.

PE As I understand it, that applies to everyone. So the people working as artists are people who have resisted the forms of determination in our capitalist system, and feel they are maintaining this difference?

JR Ultimately, emancipation always consists in stepping out of the role one has been assigned, and showing an ability characterized by the fact that it's a shared one.

PE   I think this perspective is the reason for the success of your work among young people.

JR   I hope so!

PE   Because they feel threatened by having to assume roles that are assigned to them, and which they don't want.

JR   Naturally emancipation isn't the emancipation of a particular class. That's essentially the important thing.

PE   Emancipation forges ahead in aesthetic activities, but also in . . .

JR   . . . all social activities, of course.

PE   . . . all social activities that aren't yet fixed. That's where the idea of communism being presented once again today as a response to the symptoms of economic and social crisis in Western capitalist democracies – by Alain Badiou or Slavoj Žižek, for example – differs completely from your idea of emancipation.

JR   I'm not entirely sure what the idea of communism is. I did take part in a colloquium on the subject,[8] but it wasn't defined there. I don't see a communism of the future being defined positively in these colloquia, these texts. I think that if there's a communist idea that makes sense as an idea, it's the idea of a world based on these practices of emancipation, that is, the idea that there is an intelligence shared by everyone, no matter who they are, which one must try to put into action. I can understand the communist idea as the idea of putting a joint capability into action, in the face of a world whose hierarchy is based on the difference between those who know and those who don't, those who pursue their humble work in their corner and those who have a view of the whole. Can that really determine the programme of a political party or an organized vision of the future today? I don't know.

PE   But that has nothing to do with the project of realizing an idea from the nineteenth century.

JR   No, it actually doesn't. I think there are several approaches. There's certainly this idea of a joint capability that organizes the shared world, and there are historical models of communism based on the idea that social evolution creates the material foundation for communism. From the moment when people were confronted with the historical evidence that social evolution doesn't create the historical conditions for a realization of the joint capability of its own accord – what happens to communism then? I confess that I don't know. Today one can say that one has to be a communist, because capitalism is truly ugly. Agreed. But that doesn't envision any plan for a future society. Among the authors who follow this idea today, I haven't yet found a single plan that goes in this direction.

PE   Not even a start?

JR   No, nobody is developing a strategy for developing a future society. That's what I tried to say at that colloquium: in a sense, Badiou doesn't say any more about communism than I do. Certainly one can say that his communism is likewise based on the idea of a shared intelligence, even if he turns it into a Platonic idea. But beyond that idea, is the flag he waves anything more than a flag? How does it work? What purpose does it serve? What does it demand for the future? I really don't know.

PE Does your description of this approach to re-establishing the idea of communism allow for the idea that its way of functioning might follow the logic of the representative regime?

JR I don't think so, because the communism they propose is a kind of symbol. It's not part of a logic that could show us how to achieve communism. I think this communism remains aesthetic, in the sense that it remains a notion these authors have about coexistence, and isn't at all a plan for the realization of a communist society.

PE A question we haven't yet discussed is the history of communism, which I think mustn't be passed over. In my opinion, we're making it too easy for ourselves if we cling to the idea that there was a flawed realization of communism. The only justification for re-establishing the idea of communism is this 'communist experience', which is opposed to a politics of representation. All other forms have been corrupted.

JR   Restoring the honour of the term 'communism' entails remembering all the crimes that were committed in the name of communism, as well as a comparison with all crimes committed in the name of democracy, humanism and civilization. Essentially, it's the idea of a balance – one draws the balance of the crimes in order to say that ultimately everyone committed some, and consequently all that is meaningless. I don't particularly like these balance-drawing arguments. What's more interesting is to uncover the potentials – of both the democratic and the communist forms – to realize a joint capability. That's more interesting than focusing on the criticisms. Some people want to revive the communist idea as a response to this democracy, which is used to justify military interventions and invasions like in Iraq. That ultimately leads to re-valorizing communism as a historical reality with the justification that democracy too has been guilty of crimes. That kind of justification is uninteresting. What matters is to reveal the emancipatory core in all forms that one has experienced.

Second Conversation

PE The plan was to outline your development in the first part, to clarify a few important concepts in your critical thought, and then to deal with your current perspective on politics and aesthetics, which differs from the traditional understandings of these concepts. But first I'd like to return to a question about the sensual, more precisely to your concept of the 'division of the sensual'.[9] It's a very important concept for you, and one that doesn't fit into the traditional distinction between the sensual and the intelligible.

JR It was important to me to say that the sensual doesn't exist as something general, but rather that everything which exists is always a construction or a configuration of the sensual. With reference to Kant, for example, one can say that the *Critique of Pure Reason* develops a particular conception of the sensual and the *Critique of Judgement* another. In other words, the sensual does not exist as such. What I call the 'division of the sensual' isn't a matter of two terms, the given material aspect on the one hand and the intelligible on the other. What one can call 'the sensual' is from the outset a connection, is always a particular relationship between sense and sense. In French, as in German, one uses the same word (*sens*) to refer both to what is sensually given and to the sense of this given, its interpretation. This first point is important for what I call a division of the sensual. We don't have two terms, for example a thing that is given and an authority that reflects on this given; rather, one always has a pre-existing, a priori relationship between a thing that is perceived and a sense that is ascribed to it.

The second aspect, which is very important to me, is that the way one defines the relationship between sense and sense, between the perceptible and the thinkable, is always also a way of dividing up human individuals or groups by assigning abilities or inabilities to them which concern their place. That's why the traditional philosophical question, 'What is thought?', is actually always a way of deciding who can think. If, for example, one sets up a hierarchy between the different parts of the soul, as Plato does, one is already deciding who can think. An idea of the sensual and an idea of thinking always act as the precondition determining who is afforded the ability to think. A division of the sensual is never just a form of phenomenological constitution of the perceptible, the utterable and the thinkable. It is always also a form of hierarchy among sentient beings. When Aristotle says that politics is the concern of those with language, as opposed to animals, which only have a voice, one can immediately see that there is a division here. When he goes on to say that slaves understand language but do not possess it, one has the idea of a hierarchy, an allocation of human beings that is always based on a distinction between faculties of perception, faculties of the sensual and faculties of the intellect. Whenever I've spoken about the way in which politics or aesthetics represent a particular allocation of the sensual, I've always emphasized the constitution of a thinking in this subject area. This constitution is always also a form of declaration about who has the ability to perceive and think these subjects, and who doesn't.

PE   So the division of the sensual also encompasses the construction of what one calls social distinction?

JR   Yes, one can say that social distinctions and hierarchies are, in a sense, distinctions between the sensual and material faculties of those on the one side and those on the other. In my commentary on Plato's *Republic* I emphasized that Plato thinks workers and artisans should stay in their place for two reasons: firstly, because nature has given them this or that talent, not another; and secondly, because the work doesn't wait.

In a sense, space and time are constructed from the outset not as containers or empty directions, but already as a way of dividing creatures. It's a form of social allocation that differs from sociological distinctions, or distinctions between individuals according to their economic situation. My thought, fundamentally speaking, is that there's a level of sensual experience where the identity ascribed to individuals and groups is, at the same time, a configuration of space and time which they enter, and an allocation of their abilities and inabilities. I think the constitution of politics is based a priori on these forms, on this allocation, and all regimes for identifying art are connected to modifications of this allocation.

PE   So it's really a fundamental concept!

JR   Yes, for me it's a fundamental concept that stands in opposition to a certain kind of Marxist hierarchy that has the economic at the bottom, then the social, above that the political, and finally the ideological at the top. In a sense, the economic, the social, the political and the ideological are quantities in an allocation, in a division of the sensual. In the Marxist theory of ideology there's an idea that people are oppressed because they're not aware of the social machinery, because ideology ensures that they see things in false ways. This schema presupposes that there is a kind of power which presents itself to its subjects only as a fantastic semblance, and hence that there is a producer of illusions. I don't agree with that. It's not that there's the law of the system, and on top of that a system of illusion which conceals this law. There's an assignment of creatures to particular places. The people know very well that they're being exploited; it's not a matter of attaining an awareness of that exploitation in order to escape it. The problem is how to change one's sensual universe and one's universe of perception. In my analysis of the problematics of emancipation, I showed that it's not just a question of freeing oneself of illusions, of gaining consciousness to change one's situation, but of changing one's sensual universe.

PE   Could we now return from here to the question of how you define aesthetics and politics?

JR   The basis of politics is a system of relationships which implies that there are things which are considered communal. Differently put, politics presupposes that one constructs a sensual universe in which there are things, problems and matters that are seen as communal matters, which are the concern of the community, not simply private matters. Let's take the area I examined, the history of the workers. One can say that politics in this area begins where, for example, the workers say that an employment contract isn't something that should be negotiated between two individuals, but rather a concern of the community that should be decided communally, that there is a collective which debates with a collective, and that this debate is a public matter. The birth of the strike consists in saying that the level of the wage paid for a particular number of hours isn't subject to a private relationship between two individuals, but rather a public matter to be dealt with publicly. That's one example. Politics begins at the moment when a certain number of private things become communal things. That's the fundamental principle underlying the modern revolutions: what used to be a matter for monarchs is now a matter for everyone. That's one point.

Another point is that one declares that certain individuals, certain groups, are capable or incapable of dealing with community matters. Regarding this, I recalled the distinction between active and passive people, which has nothing to do with whether one does more or is more active, but rather constitutes a distinction between people who live in different sensual universes. If one looks at universal suffrage in modern Western states, one can see that it demands abandoning this division between active and passive people. Even during the French Revolution, there were many republican constitutions that distinguished between active and passive citizens. The active citizens were the people who could pay taxes. The passive people were those who weren't subject to taxation because they simply lived from the labour of their hands and owned no property. Roughly speaking, the active citizens were the property-owning ones. So there was the idea – which also appears in the first American constitutions – that only those who own property and have some-thing to defend should take part in politics. Or let's take the issue of women: it's well known that women were excluded from suffrage for a very long time because they were considered depend-ent on their husbands or their fathers. As politics is made by free subjects, women, who weren't free subjects, couldn't vote. It's very important to determine who is involved in directing com-munal matters, and who isn't; that presupposes a decision about the quasi-physical identity and sensual faculties of individuals or groups.

So politics exists first of all in keeping with a particular allocation of the sensual, and exists in so far as one presupposes that there is an ability shared by everyone, no matter who they are, beyond all the abilities that are specific to the professor, the doctor, the scholar, the strategist. There's a joint ability shared by everyone. So in that sense, one can say that politics is based on an allocation of the sensual.

PE In the sense that this allocation determines access or non-access to politics?

JR There are two opposing principles here. There is the principle of what I've called the 'police', where the joint ability is actually reserved for certain people. There are those who work with their hands, who earn their personal living, and there are those who deal with the concerns of the community. So the principle of police is a principle of allocating places that attributes abilities according to identity: workers have the ability to do things with their hands, women have the ability to bear and bring up children, but the educated, enlightened property owner has the ability to deal with the concerns of the community. That's the principle that I call police, whereas real politics takes place where one opposes this with an ability that's the ability of all, no matter who they are. That's the basis for the idea of a political government in the true sense, which isn't simply the government of the head of the family, the chief or the scholar. In Plato one repeatedly finds the notion of the politician as a shepherd. To me, that notion is the principle of police, not politics. The true principle of politics is that there is no shepherd, no special competency, but rather a competency of all, no matter who they are. What one usually calls the political is, in reality, the conflict between two antagonistic principles – the principle of police and the principle of politics.

PE   Can one conceive of a politics in the part of society that's excluded?

JR   It's not a matter of defining the parts of society where politics exists. I think there are two levels here. One fundamental level is the basis for the idea of politics, the idea of a competency of all, no matter who they are, in contrast to the competency of the doctor, the sage, the chief, the father of a family and so forth. Now, naturally one could say that what we call politics is actually a form of conflict between the principle of politics in general and the fact that the forms of government, the forms of leadership in communal matters, are actually claimed by small minorities for themselves, minorities that purport to know: by experts, elders, whomever.

PE   And what about political parties?

JR   Political parties as we know them belong, one could say, to a class of people who supposedly have the specific competency to direct the concerns of the community. But for me, politics exists when there are forms of deviation from this specialization, when there is a specific power among those who have no specific power and no specific office. In the *Laws*, Plato distinguishes every possible form of power and compiles a catalogue of all existing forms of authority. Theirs is the power of the father over the children, of the old over the young, of the scholars over the ignorant, and at the end of the list is a completely incomprehensible, abstruse power: the power of destiny. It is the power of democracy as a regime in which there is no form of authority that exists in advance and determines which people should exercise power. For Plato, that's a small oddity at the end of the list. For me, on the contrary, this oddity at the end of the list is the true principle of politics, namely the existence of a power of all, no matter who they are, constantly embodied in the forms of action and the forms of assembly among those who are excluded from directing power.

PE I think I follow you now. You view that as the genealogy of power?

JR Politics is fundamentally tied to the division of even the *idea* of power. If one takes another look at Plato's list, there's a whole series of powers that are somehow tied to a natural form of superiority: the scholar knows, the ignorant person does not, the father is the father, the son is the son, the old man is old, the young boy is young. There are all sorts of powers that are self-legitimized, you could say. That could just as easily be the archaic power of the patriarch or the modern knowledge of the expert. All these archaic and modern powers belong to a system of self-legitimization, that is, there is already a pre-existing relationship in which there is a more powerful and a less powerful party. But there is a point where a power appears that doesn't belong to this system, precisely because such a division – a division between those who are naturally destined for power and those who are naturally destined to be ruled – doesn't exist. That's the democratic principle.

PE Is this democratic principle a principle that's no longer natural?

JR Yes, a principle that no longer has a natural justification, that's not self-legitimized. This principle is the only basis for the existence of a political governance as such. When patriarchs rule, one has a patriarchal government, not a political one. Really, democracy isn't a specific regime; it's the democratic subject that provides the basis for the existence of politics in the first place. That's why, when one looks at our governments, our Western systems, one sees that they rest on a twofold legitimacy: the people possess the principle of power, and the small groups of political experts, bankers and so on who exercise power are obliged to do so in the name of the people, and at once in the name of the competency which they supposedly have and the people do not have. So we are really operating within systems of dual legitimacy and a competition between legitimacies. Take the example of the European constitution or the contract for the European Union, on which the French populace was consulted – as it's a contract between peoples, one asks the people to decide. The entire political class – the right and the left – agreed that one should vote 'yes' in the referendum on the contract. The result of the referendum was 'no' by a large majority. This 'no' led to the negotiation of a new contract. The president at the time, Sarkozy, was asked whether there would be a new referendum, and he decided that there wouldn't be one, because contracts between peoples are a serious matter that shouldn't be determined by the chance results of a plebiscite. So here we see two opposing legitimacies: on the one hand, the legitimacy of the people which is unavoidable as an authority if one wants to be considered a democracy; and on the other hand, a legitimacy that one invokes when the people don't make the right decision, which consists in having important things decided by serious people – in this case, people who know that this contract is necessary. And so the contract is signed, despite being rejected by the people.

PE So you're not surprised to find these two principles at work?

JR No, one sees the tension between two systems of legitimacy exposed, as it were.

PE Are these two principles constitutive for democracy?

JR There's a form of legitimacy which is democratic in the true sense, but at the same time, I would say it's constantly interwoven with a form of oligarchic legitimacy which states that only the serious people can take care of the serious things.

PE So democracy isn't a form of politics . . .

JR No, it's not a constitutional form, but rather the actual principle of politics. It causes politics to exist. If one looks back at Plato again, one sees that he considers the king as a shepherd to be the right model, the shepherd who cares for his flock, and that democracy is something wayward by comparison. But to me, this deviation is politics itself, and it ensures that there is a political government, not simply governments consisting of priests, scholars, patriarchs and so on.

PE   Does this mean that the dictatorships of the twentieth century were a return to this Platonic principle?

JR   One's never dealing with a completely pure model; all models are interwoven. But yes, one can say that there is a return to the model of the shepherd who looks after his flock.

PE   I'm interested in the dimensions of democracy. Are the dictatorships of Stalin or Hitler deviations? Do they stand outside of politics, if one defines politics as democracy?

JR   As I say, one's never dealing with completely pure models where one can say where politics is and where police is. But, at the same time, these dictatorships constitute the maximum distance from politics because they try to create a kind of relationship between the power and the people in which the power lies in the hands of an authority which embodies the people in the form of the *Führer*, in the form of the party of the avant-garde and so forth. One can say that dictatorships rest on a negation of politics, with the constitution of a space that's no longer a political space.

PE   That's important, because even today there are some who wish to solve economic problems through dictatorial and authoritarian regimes.

JR   That tendency does exist, as an extreme manifestation of the rule of police over politics. Take the case of China. What's notable about it is that here one has an example of a capitalist force ruled by a communist party, where the existence of a communist party – along with the election of a communist party and the supposed dictatorship of the proletariat – becomes, in a sense, the ideal instrument for regulating capitalism. There's the possibility of suppressing workers' rights and a large number of other rights that constitute obstacles to the rule of capitalism. Here we have the paradox that the strongest capitalist power, which we also acknowledge as the most remarkable, is controlled by a communist party.

PE   There are voices which praise this model as the solution to our problems.

JR I don't know if there are people who say that; but this paradox certainly shows that there's no natural connection whatsoever between capitalism and democracy, as some would like to think.

PE Let's talk about some of the more recent social movements that have formed in the last few years – I'm thinking the protest movement Occupy, for example, which resists social and economic inequality, or of the revolts in the Arab world that were welcomed euphorically as the 'Arab Spring', although this initial enthusiasm has largely given way to disillusionment. At any rate, there are movements initiated by people who have been excluded from the political system until now, and are trying to develop new forms of discourse, new ways to show themselves, to address the concerns of the community or to be included in the regulation of communal matters. How do you see these phenomena, and what are the prospects for new social movements today?

JR I would say that there's something here which reminds us of what democracy means. It's interesting that these demonstrations have targeted both dictatorial regimes and so-called parliamentary or representative democracies. Even if young people in Spain are in an entirely different situation from those in Tunisia, there's still something like a shared feeling of being the victim of an economic system and of being excluded from the forms of collective decision-making. That takes on completely different forms, far more extreme ones in Tunisia and Egypt than in Spain, the USA or other countries where this movement of the 'outraged' arose. In all of these cases one could observe the demonstration of a people who are no longer represented by the head of state or by the state, the government or the parliament, but are instead the people of all, no matter who they are. What was noticeable about the Arab Spring and the movement of the 'outraged' was that one was no longer dealing with a people consisting of social groups, of identifiable classes; instead, there was a form of shared condition that affected all these people. The protesters included the simple Tunisian merchant whom the police prevented from doing his work, as well as European university graduates who have PhDs but no jobs. I think a general precarity is developing that's tied to the economic system, but is also a form of transversal subjectification of existing social identities. That comes very close to what I call the manifestation of those with no part (*sans-part*). They can be very poor or not so poor; they can be Spanish or American graduates, or unemployed Tunisians or Egyptians. I would say they're all involved in the same general conditions of capitalism today, and emphasizing the same distance from the system. They're also emphasizing this same ability to be there, to remind people of their presence and to emphasize that they too are the people, that it's their turn to speak and that they demand a say in running their country and world events. That's the interesting thing about the idea of 'We are the people' or 'We are the 99 per cent', because it reminds us of the foundation of politics: the opposition between two logics. On the one hand, there's an oligarchic system – I call it a police system – in which supposedly competent people control all forms of circulation, such as the circulation of cash flows or the circulation of people or, via international education agreements, the circulation of knowledge. And then there's the reality of the people who live in this system and who, for various reasons, are excluded from it or made completely precarious. They actually can't be represented anymore by so-called political parties, which are now simply parts of a state apparatus. I would say that these movements remind people of the principle of democracy, namely that there is a power among those who have no share in power or no competency. They're people who are ultimately declared incapable of dealing with the concerns of the community. It's a manifestation of democracy, especially in their opposition to our oligarchic systems, though the systems call themselves democracies.

One can say that all these movements remind people what 'democracy' really means. This brings up the problem of inscribing these movements in their time, a problem one must separate from the clichés about spontaneity and organization at all costs. What we saw in the movements in city squares was the self-assertion of a different form of people, a people of the nameless rather than the people organized by the state via the electoral process, but it's clear that the problem is how to maintain the ability to achieve this independence. The organizations that grew from this movement had to develop their own agendas, aims and forms of assembly, action, information and dissemination instead of submitting to the state and media agendas, whose temporality is shaped by the rhythm of elections and election polls. The city square movements didn't manage to create such organizations. Either their potential was exhausted or it was appropriated by organizations like Syriza in Greece or Podemos in Spain, which confined the autonomous temporality of these movements to the election calendar and the typical logic of the 'radical left', which attempts to exploit the people's disappointment with the traditional left for its own ends.

PE So we're living in a double system?

JR Yes, we're living in a double system of power in which the scales sometimes tip more to the one side, sometimes more to the other. It's obvious that the oligarchy has more weight at the moment, and that's why democracy today can only assert itself in movements that stand outside the usual forms of political representation or social movements. I think we're no longer in the realm of political parties, nor in the realm of trade union action. We're dealing with something like a manifestation of the people as such, that is, a people of the anonymous, of individuals who are all in the same situation of exclusion – though this exclusion doesn't mean they have to be poor. That's what I was trying to say when I referred to those with no part. They're persons who, to varying degrees, are effectively excluded from the system, and that system is becoming increasingly generalized.

PE   At the other end of the traditional spectrum we have the far right. Doesn't it have the same logic as those protesters? In Austria, France and elsewhere, it got thirty per cent of votes or more, it has power. How do you see this phenomenon?

JR   In the case of the French right, the Front National, we really have a combination of two phenomena. On the one side there's a radical right which holds the opinion that the traditional right isn't hard enough in its positions. On the other side there's a group whose cohesion rests on a feeling of being excluded from the system. That's especially true in France, in a presidential system with majority representation, where one can say that the system governing transitions of power is a monopoly system with two parties.

So, on the one hand, the far right is a far right, but on the other hand it's also something else, an expression of the feeling of exclusion from the system. That's why this part of the far right can recruit voters who had previously voted for socialists, communists or labour parties. I think that when the people are forgotten by the system, what results is a kind of mythology of a people of the forgotten, the uncounted, the true people, which can be exploited by the far right. These are deeply opposing forms, but ultimately they're both a consequence of the consensual system. In the case of France, one can say that the far right grew together with the consolidation of the presidential majority system, a system of alternation between two dominant parties that have the same politics, broadly speaking.

PE One can observe this tendency all over Europe.

JR Yes, it's like a caricature of the power of the democratic people, which is always excessive compared to the people as embodied by state logic. The far right responds to this with a different form of imaginary embodiment by purporting to be the 'true' people, the real people. But there's no such thing as the 'true' people, there are only ever competing constructs of a people.

PE Let's go back to the idea of a return to communism as an ethical principle. Is that a political alternative?

JR I think the starting point has to be the fact that there's no communist alternative at present. There are parties, certainly. We know that there are still communist parties in power, in Cuba, in North Korea, in China. But one sees that 'actual' communism, the kind of communism that operates in China, is the regulation of a capitalist economy by a single party. One can say that it's the rule of the capitalist class over the popular classes. That's the reality of communism today. Then there are also the Western communist parties, which are all extremely weak. The French communist party, which, together with the Italian party, was one of the great surviving communist parties in Western Europe, is now forced to hide in an alliance that calls itself Front de gauche. So there's an extreme weakness among the representatives of historical communism, which is defeated and transformed everywhere; they become capitalists, as in Russia, or hide behind other left-wing groups, as in Western Europe. Generally, one can say that the historical communist movement has virtually disappeared.

As we discussed earlier, there are people who are adopting the communist label again, but I'd say it's no more than a label, because those people have no programme whatsoever that might tell us what the communist society of the future will look like. They have no historical perspective at all, no strategy at all that leads to a future society. They simply wave a flag and say that democracy is just capitalism. They recount a long history of the crimes of capitalism in order to qualify the crimes of communism, and argue that everyone committed crimes. Because capitalism is a system of domination, exploitation and inequality, they recommend hoisting the communist flag again. I say, it's always just a flag! As I mentioned earlier, I've been to one or two colloquia whose goal was to rekindle the communist flame, and I never heard a single description of a future communism, I never saw a single outline for a programme describing how to move from capitalism in its current form to communism.

The idea of communism today consists of two basic things: firstly, the idea that capitalism is a bad and criminal system, which one can agree with, and secondly, the idea of a society that is organized for the benefit of as many people as possible by a power that expresses the ability of as many people as possible. However much certain theorists, including Badiou and Žižek, might place the communist idea in opposition to the democratic idea, there is no more to their communist idea than to the democratic idea, except that they adopt Plato's critique of democracy. They formulate the idea of communism by transforming it into a Platonic idea, into an intelligible idea that controls the democratic material. To me, this idea is no different from the idea of a power of the majority, which is based on the idea of an ability shared by as many people as possible.

PE Is there still a belief today that one should return to early Marx, the dream of a return to a humanistic communism that hasn't been compromised?

JR I don't think that anyone is espousing the idea that one should return to early rather than late Marx. There was a time, during the fifties and the sixties, when this idea preoccupied communist movements.

PE   At the time that was to avoid the dictatorship of the proletariat.

JR   Yes, it was the idea that one could retrieve a form of Marxist humanism, a form of humanist striving with which one could oppose the system of power confiscation that had existed in the USSR and so-called people's democracies. That got hopes up in a few Eastern countries. And there were actually hints of it in Hungary, Yugoslavia and in a few Western movements, but this 'humanitarian' Marxism was criticized and swept away by Althusserianism, by the idea that this humanist Marxism is not true Marxism, that true Marxism is a scientific Marxism. I think that existed at the time, but I don't really see anything of the kind today. So I don't think that the current will to return to communism is based on the idea of a humanist Marx in contrast to a scientific and dictatorial Marx. I think that today, Marx's thought is being taken as a kind of block again. And what lives on as the core of Marx's thought? Essentially the conception of class struggle. I think an important aspect of this revival of Marxist thought is to say that what's described in terms of the necessary, inescapable global situation is in reality a state of class struggle. I think it's important to remind people of that today – against the predominant analyses, which refer to a historical necessity. Since the fall of communism, the Marxist argument of historical and economic necessity has, broadly speaking, been adopted by the bourgeoisie, by the ruling power, except that instead of claiming that universal history leads to communism, it declares that it leads to the triumph of the market. One can see how the old Marxist arguments of economic necessity, the necessity of breaking through the old barriers, were actually taken up by capitalism, by the ruling classes and the ruling ideology, to say that there's an inescapable necessity: the necessity of the free market, the absolute power of the market.

Regarding that, I think it's important to foreground those analyses which say that the world situation isn't the result of a necessary global evolution, but a state of class struggle. It's clear that the ruling classes, the worldwide alliance of the ruling classes, are in a position of extreme strength, but one shouldn't mistake this world-view for historical reality. So I think that Marxist thought plays an important part in breaking up what's being sold to us as the inevitable evolution of the world.

PE The concept of class had a very clear definition in Marxist theory that doesn't apply to the current situation. If one uses the concept of class, one can't really understand a phenomenon like the global precariat. Perhaps one can't use it at all to describe the real social divisions?

JR One has to take into account that there are many interpretations of the class concept. There's the strictly sociological interpretation of classes, for example. But the idea of class struggle contains the basic thought that the classes are defined by the struggle itself. The proletariat, for example, isn't just the class of all those who are exploited by capitalism. The proletariat is, quite fundamentally, the class of those who can form an alternative power to capitalist rule. The idea of class struggle doesn't state that first of all there are classes, and then they enter the struggle; it states that there's a power system and there are forces which fight against this power system.

Of course, if one thinks of the 'proletariat' in the sense of a mass of workers who get up and leave the Renault factory, one can spend a long time looking for it today; one won't find it in our society. But this doesn't mean that the proletariat doesn't exist elsewhere; these giant factories don't exist in France anymore, nor in Austria or Spain. They're in China, Singapore, Korea, almost everywhere in the Far East, sometimes also in Eastern Europe. That's why people say that this class of proletarians doesn't exist anymore; yet it's clear that it certainly does still exist but in a new part of the world: there one finds this traditional proletarian class, including the familiar forms of exploitation. If one looks at the slums of Mumbai, for example, one recognizes forms of capitalist exploitation – starting with labour at home – that recall the forms of exploitation which existed in nineteenth-century England and are described by Marx. So, on the one hand, there's a kind of traditional proletariat in countries where the conditions for struggle are very difficult, especially in China – because if there's one country with a proletariat of the old kind, it's surely China. But this proletariat lacks all the means of organization and struggle that were available to the proletariats of Western countries in the nineteenth and twentieth centuries. On the other hand, in the countries where we live, there's a kind of fragmentation which is no longer focused on the masses of workers organized in the factory, the business and the trade unions. It's a fragmented condition, but a shared one nonetheless. That's why I believe in the importance of these new democratic movements, large parts of which are expressions of this precariat. So there's class struggle, first of all in the sense that there's a ruling class which carries out the class struggle, and does so very systematically. Let's take a look at what's happening at the European level: the EU Council dictates to the Greek government that they have to lower wages and cut social benefits. There were elections, a new government, a referendum – the Greek people's rejection of these measures was confirmed repeatedly. But the Troika imposed its will, the joint will of the European government and the financial institutions. There's a manifest praxis of class struggle, and today it's the capitalists who are taking the initiative in that struggle.

The problem today isn't that there are no classes anymore. The capitalist international exists, it holds the power. On this side there's class struggle, there are no problems here. What's difficult is the organization of the precarious class. The problem is also the relationship between this precarious class and the traditional working class, which is far away, which one doesn't see anymore, but which exists. And thirdly, there are masses of migrants crossing borders in search of possibilities for a better life, and of refugees fleeing from war and oppression in Syria and elsewhere. So I think there's a fierce class struggle today, with a well-placed class on one side, the ruling class, and on the other side, elements that don't succeed in coming together as a class.

PE That's very interesting. If the communist position refers to a traditional concept, doesn't that prevent a search for new concepts? Isn't the resurgence of communism, of the communist idea, an obstacle to the development of new ideas for a way out of the crisis?

JR So far we've only examined one aspect of this communist revival. But one shouldn't forget that there are other aspects to this revival too, and they're connected to the development of a new make-up of the different classes. If one considers the whole tradition of Italian workerism, the reflections by Toni Negri and Michael Hardt, one can see an attempt to base communism once more on the idea of an evolution, a transformation of status and the relationship between the classes. Concepts like the precariat, for example, were first advanced in the Italian workerist tradition in an attempt to follow the transformations of the old working class. That led especially to deliberations on the idea of the intellectual worker in immaterial capitalism, that is, on the idea that immaterial capitalism produces a new class which possesses instruments of collective intelligence.

I think there's also another problem: knowing how to conceive of the relationship between the present and the future. According to the old Marxist model, capitalism creates the conditions for its own removal – the famous formulation about capitalism producing its own gravediggers. So one sees how workerist thinking remains somewhat tied to the schema in which capitalism brings about its own ruin. This attempt to envisage the status of the proletariat using a specific category – that of the so-called intellectual worker – is extremely double-edged, because what's described there could just as easily be a working class that's completely integrated into the system. So I think one mustn't forget that the capitalism of material production continues to exist, and that the fact that we hardly see it in Paris or Rome doesn't mean that it doesn't exist in China, Malaysia or India. That's the first point. Secondly, I think there's no necessity for immaterial production to beget a category of workers that holds some form of communist future. In other words, I don't think that the ways of collectivizing capitalist power automatically beget any form of future communism. The fact that there are numerous businesses today in which the people working at the computers own the means of production, in a certain sense, doesn't mean that this creates the conditions for a communist class of the future in which the people own their means of production. No, I think the two things are very different. Furthermore, there are also two different lines of thought within this workerist tradition itself. There's a line of thought that one could call traditionally Marxist in which capitalism, by transforming itself, brings about the conditions for a new society, which means that communism already exists inside of capitalism. That's a thesis I consider radically wrong. And there's another version of this where capitalism doesn't produce a class of immaterial workers, but rather a class of producers of material or immaterial riches who have no control at all over the totality of the system, and no say at all in public matters. Behind the fantasy of the intellectual worker of the future, I think, lies the reality of the precarious worker – who, as I said, could just as easily be the Tunisian merchant or the Spanish or Portuguese computer scientist. At this point, it's conceivable that there's genuinely a milieu in which not only forms of struggle but also forms of life could develop slightly outside the system. The concept of 'exodus' was famously successful for a while in the workerist tradition; this was tied to the idea of the possibility of autonomization in the class of immaterial workers produced by capitalism. I think that at this point one comes back to the old choice: either one thinks that the future is created by the development specific to capitalist production and organization – an idea whose historical failure is proven – or one believes that any departure from the system results not from the development of the system itself, but from the development of all the forms of resistance and autonomy that one attains in relation to the system. But that, as we know, is an old debate about the issue of autonomy. To what extent do forms of autonomy come about now through forms of work, and do they really come about?

I think it's never the system itself that creates the conditions for this. For there to be autonomous forces which possibly become forces of the future, these forces have to produce their own life system, thought system and information system, even their own institutions. And that, if we return to the question of the more recent social movements, is where the problem lies. Are these movements condemned to being simply a kind of official declaration that says 'We're here', or are these movements capable of initiating a kind of autonomous development, creating their own forms of discussion, their own forms of life, their own economic organization, their own institutions of information and knowledge? That's the real question for me. I think the model of a necessary development from one regime to another, one system to another, is obsolete. What's still imaginable, if not the development of a kind of autonomous system of forms of the future in the present? That's essentially what interested me, and what I examined historically via the problematics of workers' emancipation. It's the development of power forms that are autonomous in relation to the prevailing system. As we know, that was very pronounced in the European labour movement, but was stamped out by the communist parties on the one hand and the capitalist powers on the other. Could that exist today, now, under the new conditions of labour division, of class division? That's the question that arises. And I don't know if there's much more to say about it.

PE Can we now connect this question of the possibility of developing autonomous forms of power with your second line of thought, with your reflections on aesthetics and the analysis of artistic practices? If I understand you correctly, artistic activity can have this ability to establish new, autonomous worlds.

JR In my opinion, art as such doesn't have a purpose. I don't think that art as such necessarily has a political purpose, but it's certain that under the conditions of the aesthetic regime and the conditions of contemporary art, we're no longer dealing with the old relationship between art and politics, where people asked themselves how artists should take part in the political struggle. We're no longer in the old problematics of commitment, as in Sartre's day, but rather in a system where what we call art has many forms of existence that are completely heterogeneous. There are people who paint, who paint abstract or representational pictures . . . and there are countless people who use different means – installations, photography, video – to create something like a different visibility of the world we live in, and other systems for circulating images, circulating information. One can see very clearly that this isn't limited to individual artist-activists. Whatever international exhibition one goes to – Biennale, documenta or others – there's a whole range of forms that essentially amount to a circulation of information. Many things that happen in the world are familiar to us less through the official information routes, not through television and newspapers, but through the work of artists who investigate and document all sorts of things. In a sense, many artists have taken over and transformed the tasks of sociologists, journalists or even political agitators. That's very important, I think. With the Arab Spring, for example, one assumes that there is a connection – albeit an indirect one – between the emergence of these movements and the work of many artists in the Middle East and North Africa, who were trying to create anew the visibility of what was happening in their countries and questioning the traditional depictions of the rulers and the victims, or of the relationship between society and religion. And the type of activist one sees at the centre of recent protest movements is also the same as that one encounters in the major artistic fora, the major international art exhibitions. A kind of milieu is developing of people who stand between the artist and the political activist, who try to redesign the visibility of the divisions of today's world.

PE The artists who don't have any success on the art market of the capitalist system have long formed a precariat. There are many artists in this area.

JR Here one has to take several things into account. There are indeed unsuccessful artists who belong to the precariat. In the nineteenth century, whenever there were revolutionary movements, the right wing claimed they were led by writers without readers, artists without buyers, or prostitutes without customers. There was always this equation of unsuccessful writers or bad artists with discontented persons expressing their discontent.

But there's something else that runs deeper, I think, which is connected to the change in artistic forms and practices. Today the word 'art' refers to extremely varied things. One immediately thinks of the artists Jeff Koons, Damien Hirst and so forth, the darlings of the market, but the art world doesn't only consist of successful and unsuccessful artists. It consists of a multitude of places and different activities. Thus a single art school, let's say the Goldsmith College in London, produces Damien Hirst as well as all sorts of people who, without being artists in the true sense, become independent exhibition curators or professors at art academies or take on intermediate functions whose tendency is to blur the image of the artist. I think a certain blurring of the image of the artist, which ensures that there isn't politics on one side and the artist on the other, with the function of illustrating it – as with Fernand Léger and the communist party – is an important phenomenon. There's really a very important area of indistinguishability between the means of artistic practice and those of politics. And one must always take into account that today's artists do a wide range of things. They're not simply artists who have varyingly favourable relationships with the market; they work with all sorts of institutions. Many artists also teach, and teaching means that one's involved in all the systems of educational reforms, such as the Bologna Process. Artists and artistic practices are integrated into entirely different processes from the traditional ones and those restricted to selling art. The membership of artists in a form of precariat isn't the same thing as the Bohème of the nineteenth century. It's something completely different in so far as artists also work on social conditions and are the carriers of social struggles. Look at the struggles of freelance artists, for example – that is, all those whose social security depends on working for a number of hours as an actor, say, but also as staff members at art academies, as dancing instructors or orchestral musicians. So there are all kinds of social occupations and forms of subjectification that are brought together in the concept of the artist. Many musicians in major orchestras are also freelance artists, as are many people who work in television. There's a whole category of people who are not only involved in the art market, but also depend on normal employment and precarious working conditions, part-time work and so forth. Many artists are in this situation, as is the university lecturer with a part-time job or no permanent position. So on the one hand, there's the integration of a large number of artists into what one could call the conditions of this new precariat, and on the other, there's the transformation of artistic practices themselves. What artists do with words, photos, pictures, videos or installations very often aims no longer to create a work of art as such, but a veritable system of documentation, information and construction of the visibility and conceivability of the world.

What I said about the relationship between the perceptible, the utterable and the thinkable is also significant in contemporary art. Many contemporary art forms are forms of the relationship between different media that question the relationship between a visual form, words and the thought regime in which these visual forms and words can go together. Think of all these forms that attempt to comment on performances and put an action or a performance into images or words. I think the forms of contemporary art are largely ways of enacting the relationships between the words, the visual forms, the images, the times and the spaces, and at the same time they create a kind of sensual fabric that reframes the visibility of labour today, for example, or the situation of migrant workers. I'm thinking of something like the film *Colossal Youth* by Pedro Costa, which is something like an attempt to reframe the figure of immigrant so that he's no longer viewed as a poor devil, but as a traveller with his own experience, his own view of the world, the new world he lives in. Think of all the ways of reframing labour that have also resulted from artistic practices, and the ways in which artists follow the redistributions of working methods. Allan Sekula's exhibitions and films, for example, show how American factories are transported to Korea or China. So while the typical opinion is that there are no more factories, one suddenly has these fairly unspectacular photographs or films that show a factory in the USA being dismantled and loaded onto a ship, and then rebuilt in Korea. This renders visible a dominant form of capitalist circulation which is concealed both by the shipping spaces full of colourful, silent containers and by the talk of production becoming immaterial. That's just one of many examples. I'm also thinking of the work of Lebanese artists who are trying to reshape the visibility of their country by not revelling in misery and showing ruins and victims, but instead by being interested in changing the landscape, in the question of depicting what has disappeared, or by inverting the typical question and looking at what the war has done to pictures materially, quite concretely, because many pictures vanished during the civil war, couldn't be developed or even taken, because there were no film rolls (this was before the digital age). In this way, art no longer treats war as an object of representation. The two questions merge in one and the same work about the visible and the invisible. So there's work to achieve a change of perspective, which I consider very important. It's one example next to a thousand others showing that the manifold ways in which artists put words and images together suddenly interfere with the consensual view that's constructed by governments and the dominant media.

PE Even if a large number of artists are in a precarious situation that's not of their own choosing, they did choose one thing: not to be reduced to the condition of the worker. So their role within the precariat is important because they, unlike other persons and groups in the precariat, are active.

JR Yes, that's undoubtedly important, because it presupposes abandoning a traditional thought-figure of the relationship between the artist and politics that's focused on the question of whether the artist should commit to something or not. Today we're in situations where this question doesn't arise, because the artist has de facto become a part of a particular condition resulting from the current power system, and because the topic which so many artists address in their work, broadly speaking, is information, the construction of the images of our world. In that sense, we're completely outside the traditional divisions between the artist and society or the artist and politics – even if it exists. If a successful actor raises money to help with a natural disaster or in a crisis situation, or sets up their own charitable foundation, one's probably dealing with the traditional figure of the artist who champions a cause. But that's something which, compared to the other figure, has very much moved to the background: the figure of the artist who committed within a form of a social network and in a particular relationship with the image and text.

PE   So for you it's new milieus, new life experiences, that give hope for a social change?

JR   It's not just about life experiences. There's really a dialectic: certain forms of life, like the precariat, can produce new forms of political consciousness and new forms of political expression today. Conversely, the question is whether these political forms of expression can themselves produce their own forms of life, their own forms of development. To be meaningful today, a political movement needs to have its own forms of assembly, forms of discussion, knowledge and information production; its aims must be independent of the aims of official politics, of presidential or parliamentary elections, it needs to have its own agenda and possibly develop alternative economic forms. So that's a long haul, with fluctuations, with ups and downs. Fundamentally, I believe that if there's a force which leads out of the current power system, then part of it has to grow from these new experiences of the precariat, from these new forms of labour, from these new forms of the relationship between politics and the work, of information practice, social practice, political practice. I don't know if there's any more one can say about it, but I don't think there's any future to be gained purely from the development of the system itself. The protest that has grown from the forms of life produced by the capitalist system must be able to create autonomous forms of life and resistance, forms of action that are independent of the ruling logics that we know. That's all we can say, I think. After that one can still discuss whether the democratic or the communist idea is the right flag. I think it's more the democratic than the communist idea, but naturally one can ultimately define a kind of common foundation, a common principle of these two ideas.

PE   So you do at least see a purpose in the ethical concepts that oppose the current situation?

JR I don't know if I'd call it an ethical concept, but I think it's always productive to oppose the current distribution of power by conceiving the creation of collective forms of power that embody an ability of all, no matter who they are. That's why, for me, one could say there's a kind of democratic precondition, in the sense of a creation of forms that embody this power of all, no matter who they are, in contrast to the traditional model of an avant-garde which prepares the future.

PE Thank you, Jacques.

Afterword by Peter Engelmann

Jacques Rancière is considered one of the most important thinkers of the incipient twenty-first century, one who brings together emancipatory political and aesthetic practice in a new way.

Since the 1960s, two emancipatory philosophical schools with a global presence have established themselves: postmodernism and deconstruction. What they have in common is a critique of the previously dominant Marxism as the only fulfilling conceptual edifice of emancipatory thought and action. It had divided the world into left and right, progressive and reactionary, Marxist and wrong.

The history of the communist labour movement – its organization into parties and the dictatorship of the proletariat in the socialist states – had resulted in so many victims that these could no longer be overlooked, even by the most sympathetic minds. Intra-Marxist deviations such as Maoism proved no less disastrous than the Soviet variety of Marxism.

As the communist movement was founded by a philosopher – who then became an economist – it was only consistent that the critique of the actual communist movement was directed at its theoretical core. This historical function was fulfilled by postmodernism and deconstruction, whose main concerns are the examination and critique of totalitarian thought structures as argumentative and legitimizing foundations of totalitarian politics.

The philosopher Jacques Rancière took a different, independent path early on. In meticulous historical analyses he tried to articulate approaches to emancipatory practice that had been suppressed by totalitarian party structures. After occupying a singular position in contemporary French philosophy for many years, his research brought him back into the circle of the current avant-garde of emancipatory thought, which I would like to define as the search for new possibilities of emancipatory politics by extra-political means.

If I am not mistaken, Rancière's current work is located within the main school of socio-critical thought in contemporary French philosophy, which, after the theoretical critique of Marxist ideology and its philosophical foundations, seeks to develop new forms of emancipatory politics outside the traditional field of politics via post-modernism and deconstruction. This tendency also includes the work of Alain Badiou and Jean-Luc Nancy, however profound the differences between their philosophical approaches. In this context, Rancière has taken an entirely individual approach since the 1970s, with his critique of the structuralist interpretation of Marx which he was involved in developing. From today's perspective, his research on the subjective side of emancipatory movements makes him one of the protagonists of contemporary French philosophy.

In the tableau of current socially committed and socio-critical thought in France, there seems to be less of a running thread than a number of philosophers with varying degrees of political activity working independently of one another. Quite separately and against entirely different backgrounds, Rancière, Badiou and Nancy are trying to redefine the field of political practice in order to open up new possibilities for a self-assured emancipatory politics. I see the motivation for these reflections in the insight that the history of emancipatory efforts in the form of political movements since the nineteenth century has repeatedly led to the dead end of totalitarian parties, and, wherever those parties came to power, totalitarian states.

Whereas Jacques Derrida and Jean-François Lyotard engaged more in a critique of language and discourse, Rancière's work in the 1970s was closer to Michel Foucault's analyses of institutions. His basic conviction that equality among humans was an indispensable precondition for true democracy is expressed as much in his current texts on politics and aesthetics as it was in his research on the social movements of the nineteenth century. In his books, Rancière takes a stand against a creeping erosion of democracy. He not only criticizes media intellectuals who conform to the system and show an increasing disregard for democracy, but also offers an analysis of the latest constellations and conditions for democracy after the demise of the Soviet Union.

On the one hand, there is what Rancière refers to as 'police' in the broadest sense – that is, the totality of power that dictates an order and forces individuals into it. On the other hand, there are the equals, the people with equal validity and their own interests. The political field is the conflict between these two sides. Democracy is not consensual but conflictual. In this sense, political activity is the resistance of the nameless and partless to concrete inequality.

Since the 1990s, Rancière has increasingly augmented his political-philosophical investigations with questions of aesthetics and examinations of the connection between political and artistic activities. The starting point for his reflections is a critique of artistic practice as representation, following on from Aristotle and his concept of mimesis. For Rancière, the liberation from the function of representation in modern literature and painting enabled the development of film and other artistic media.

In the last few years, however, the train of thought with which I began these remarks has emerged with increasing consistency. To be sure, Rancière's aesthetic investigations can initially stand for themselves. In connection with his critique of politics, however, they increasingly also open up an important field of emancipatory activities. They make it possible to understand artistic practices as forms of a new emancipatory politics.

I would like to take this opportunity of an editor's note to express my special thanks to Jacques Rancière, and not only for this book. When we first met in 1975, I was a DAAD[1] student in Paris and needed a recommendation from a French professor in order to continue studying there. At the time, Rancière was a professor in Vincennes, the stronghold of new French thought, where Michel Foucault taught alongside Gilles Deleuze and Félix Guattari, Hélène Cixous and Jacques Lacan. Rancière kindly gave an assessment of my work and my plans, thus contributing to the extension of my scholarship and my stay in Paris. In so doing, he enabled me to take my own very personal academic path through French

1 The DAAD, whose initials stand for *Deutscher Akademischer Austauschdienst* (German Academic Exchange Service), is an agency that offers grants both for Germans to study abroad and for students from other countries to come to Germany [trans.].

philosophy and unknowingly laid the foundation for my own philosophical commitment. French philosophy not only became the focus of my teaching work, but also contributed to the founding of the Passagen Verlag in Vienna, which was able to open a new chapter of critical thought in German-language discourse through a systematic and lasting transfer of contemporary French thought.

After focusing on a variety of research topics for some time, Rancière and I came together again a few years ago and have been vigorously exchanging philosophical and political views ever since. The result of this exchange, in addition to the translation of many of his books, is the present volume of conversations, which is intended to offer an accessible aid to understanding his thought.

Peter Engelmann

Notes

1 Louis Althusser, Étienne Balibar et al., *Reading Capital: The Complete Edition*, trans. Ben Brewster (London: Verso, 2016).

2 Jean-Yves Calvez, *La Pensée de Karl Marx* (Paris: Editions du Seuil, 1956).

3 Jacques Rancière, *Proletarian Nights: The Workers' Dream in Nineteenth-Century France*, trans. John Drury (London: Verso, 2012).

4 Jacques Rancière, *The Philosopher and His Poor*, trans. John Drury, Corinne Oster and Andrew Parker (Durham, NC: Duke University Press, 2003).

5 Jacques Rancière, *Disagreement*, trans. Julie Rose (Minneapolis: University of Minnesota Press, 1999).

6 Pierre Bourdieu, *Distinction: A Social Critique of the Judgement of Taste*, trans. Richard Nice (Cambridge, MA: Harvard University Press, 1984).

7 See Jacques Rancière, *Aisthesis: Scenes from the*